W9-DHF-437

YES YOU CAN

Published by Familius LLC, www.familius.com
PO Box 1249 Reedley, Ca 93654

Familius books are available at special discounts for bulk purchases,
whether for sales promotions or for family or corporate use.
For more information, email orders@familius.com.

Library of Congress Control Number: 2021933768

Print ISBN 9781641704687

Printed in China

Edited by Peg Sandkam
Cover art and book design by Olivia Herrick

10 9 8 7 6 5 4 3 2 1

First Edition

YES YOU CAN

OLIVIA HERRICK

MORNING & NIGHT

The affirmations in the first half of the book
are designed to be read in the morning.

The affirmations in the second half of the book
are designed to be read at night.

HOW TO USE THIS BOOK

Carry it with you for on-the-go inspiration.

Grab it instead of your phone.

Give it to a friend when you've finished,
and ask them to pass it on as well.

Keep it on your nightstand and read an affirmation
after you wake up and before you go to bed.

Take two deep breaths, open to any page,
and reflect on what is in front of you.

I AM SO GLAD YOU'RE HERE

My hope is that this book will serve as an antidote to our hurried world—a world that demands we move at an alarming pace, buried in our devices, barely coming up for air.

My hope is that this book empowers you to be:

present
patient
empathetic
reflective
at peace

And in the quiet moments when you find yourself thumbing through these pages, I hope that you see just how strong and capable you are.

Life has a funny and frustrating way of not going according to plan at times. But with an open heart, a glass-half-full outlook, and each other, we can navigate life's greatest joys and obstacles.

I'm rooting for you.

FOR MORNING

believe
that
you can

start each
day with a
grateful heart,
a sense of peace,
and sincere
hope for what
lies ahead

talk less,
listen more

DO YOUR BEST

focused

patient

optimistic

driven

hydrated

LOVE WHERE
YOU ARE

———

KNOW WHERE
YOU'RE GOING

believe that really, truly wonderful things will find their way into your life

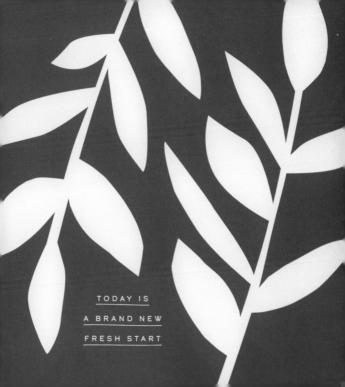

TODAY IS

A BRAND NEW

FRESH START

IT IS NEVER.
TOO LATE
TO BECOME
WHO YOU
WANT TO BE

TRY EMBRACING WHAT IS UNFOLDING IN FRONT OF YOU

RATHER THAN FOCUSING ON WHAT COULD HAVE BEEN

IF YOU WANT SOMETHING, YOU HAVE TO BE WILLING TO WORK FOR IT. DON'T SHY AWAY FROM THE WORK. EMBRACE IT. LEAN INTO IT. NOTHING GOOD COMES WITHOUT PASSION AND INTENTIONAL EFFORT.

TRUST

THE

PROCESS

HOLD
ON
TO
YOUR
HOPE

IT WON'T ALWAYS BE

EASY, BUT IT WILL

ALWAYS BE WORTH IT

GO YOUR OWN WAY

AT TIMES

THINGS

WILL GO

WRONG BUT

END UP

JUST RIGHT

YOU GOT THIS

KEEP GROWING

keep moving forward

IF YOU ARE WAITING FOR A SIGN, THIS IS IT

TODAY IS

YOUR DAY

when in doubt, keep creating

TODAY IS

A GOOD DAY

TO HAVE

A GOOD DAY

I WILL
NOT
MAKE
MYSELF
SMALL

Your
Words
Have
Power

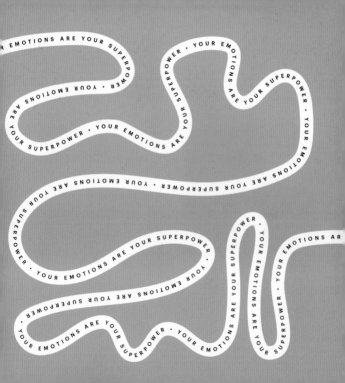

ask more
questions;
stay curious;
dig deeper

sometimes we
need to hold on;
sometimes we
need to let go

OH I THINK
IT'S GOING
TO BE A
GREAT DAY

Seen
Known
Heard
Loved

NORMALIZE

TELLING your FRIENDS

THAT YOU

LOVE THEM

LET GO OF
YESTERDAY'S
MISTAKES

you have the
heart of a lion

HALF OF LIFE
IS REFUSING TO LET
YOURSELF QUIT;

THE OTHER HALF
IS KNOWING WHEN
YOU SHOULD.

keep
learning;
keep
evolving

GOOD
GETS
BETTER

be grateful.
be adaptable.
be mindful.

you are exactly where you need to be

WONDERFUL

THEIR WAY

WILL FIND

THINGS

TO YOU

every single
person you will
encounter today
is fighting some
sort of battle.

let's default to
kindness –
not outrage.

TAKE HEART

LET GO OF WHAT IS HOLDING YOU BACK

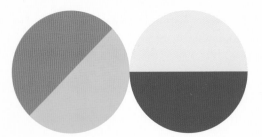

visualize this day unfolding exactly as you would like it to

REMEMBER:
IT DOESN'T
HAVE TO BE
PERFECT,
IT JUST HAS
TO BE DONE

GOOD THINGS

TAKE TIME;

DON'T

YOU DARE

GIVE UP

LIFE IS A WILD,

WONDERFUL MIRACLE —

TREAT IT AS SUCH.

WHAT KIND
OF PERSON
DO YOU WANT
TO BE TODAY?

FOR NIGHT

you are calm and capable
of what lies ahead

SOME DAYS WILL HURT AND SOME DAYS WILL HEAL

HARD WORK IS A FORM OF SELF-CARE

I WOULD GO

ANYWHERE

FOR YOU

BALANCE

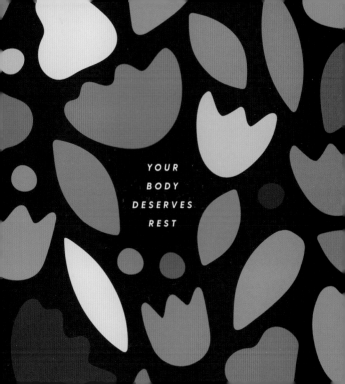

YOUR
BODY
DESERVES
REST

one day at a time

WORK HARD THEN REST

GRATEFUL FOR THE PAST

& EXCITED FOR WHAT

THE FUTURE HOLDS

see
the good

HAVE FAITH.
STAY STRONG.
PRESS ON.

WHEN IT  GETS

TOUGH,  BE STRONG

it is a gift to be
alive at this very
moment in time

LET GO

OF RESULTS

BEING YOUR

ONLY MEASUREMENT

OF SUCCESS

pause for
a moment and
acknowledge
just how far
you have come

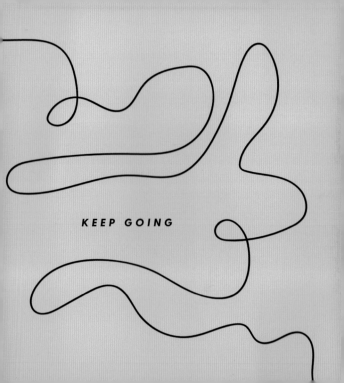

KEEP GOING

TAKE A
DEEP
BREATH

WHAT IS HOLDING YOU BACK?

CHERISH THE PRESENT

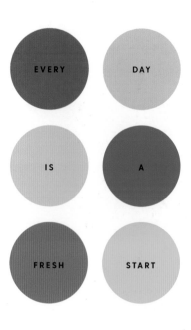

YOU WERE
BORN
FOR THIS

THE JOURNEY IS NEVER LINEAR

you are closer than you were yesterday

failure is
an important
part of
the process

GIVE THANKS
FOR THE HERE
AND THE NOW

breathe

it in and

let it go

DOESN'T HAVE TO BE PERFECT TO BE WONDERFUL • IT DOESN'T HAVE TO BE PERFECT TO BE WONDERFUL • IT DOESN'T HAVE TO BE PERFECT TO BE WONDERFUL • IT DOESN'T HAVE TO BE PERFECT TO BE WONDERFUL • IT DOESN'T HAVE TO BE PERFECT TO BE WONDERFUL • IT DOESN'T HAVE TO BE PERFECT TO BE WONDERFUL • IT DOESN'T HAVE TO BE PERF

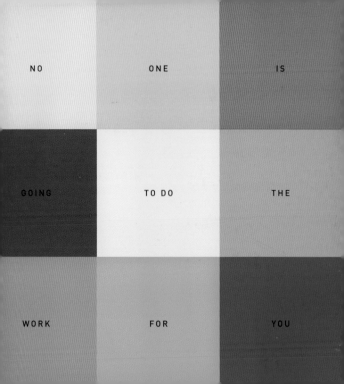

we will never
have this day again

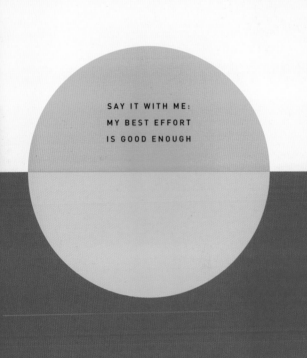

SAY IT WITH ME:

MY BEST EFFORT

IS GOOD ENOUGH

TRY TO SPEND LESS TIME WORRYING ABOUT WHAT OTHER PEOPLE ARE DOING AND THINKING AND SAYING, AND MORE TIME WORRYING ABOUT WHAT YOU CAN DO AND THINK AND SAY TO MAKE THE WORLD A BETTER AND BRIGHTER PLACE

know

when you need to

let go

WHAT CAN YOU DO TONIGHT TO PREPARE FOR A BETTER TOMORROW?

YOU CAN

&

YOU WILL

take care of yourself

It won't always work out, and that is okay.

YOU

CAN'T

CHOOSE

WHAT

YOU

FEEL

STOP
DOUBTING
WHAT
YOU ARE
CAPABLE OF

happiness requires acknowledging that life is a delicate dance of both joy and sorrow

*HAVE
FAITH
IN YOUR
LIFE*

WHERE
YOU ARE ⟶ WHERE
TODAY   YOU WANT
        (A LIFELONG JOURNEY)   TO BE

gratitude

hydration

nature

friendship

collaboration

mindfulness

sunshine

purpose

love

YOU ARE
WORKING SO
HARD & IT ISN'T
EASY, BUT JUST
SO YOU KNOW,
I THINK YOU'RE
DOING GREAT

WHATEVER

FEELS RIGHT

TO YOU

IS THE RIGHT

THING TO DO

EMBRACE THE MYSTERY

YOU CAN DO BIG BRAVE THINGS

tomorrow

will

be better

IT
WON'T
ALWAYS
BE THIS
WAY

good things
are going
to happen

Calm Your Heart

Calm Your Mind

CONSIDER THIS

PERMISSION TO

CHANGE YOUR MIND,

THINK DIFFERENTLY,

GROW AND EVOLVE

YES *

* YOU

CAN *

ACKNOWLEDGMENTS

To B and R, the center of my world. My rock, my calm, my constant in chaos. I'm all your'n.

To my family for teaching me that empathy, curiosity, and kindness are superpowers. For showing me the value of hard work and determination. And for both tolerating and encouraging my energy, enthusiasm, and emotions.

To A, C, and E for their unconditional love and friendship. At our best and at our worst—soulmates, sisters.

To my editor, Peg, and my team at Familius—Brooke, Christopher, Carlos, and Kate. Thank you for believing in me, cheering me on, and inviting me to the table.

ABOUT THE AUTHOR

Olivia Herrick is a graphic designer based in the Twin Cities of Minnesota, best known for her playful, vibrant, and positive artwork. Though you will often find her glued to her computer at her studio, Olivia finds her greatest inspiration in the great outdoors.

ABOUT FAMILIUS

Visit Our Website: www.familius.com

Familius is a global trade publishing company that publishes books and other content to help families be happy. We believe that the family is the fundamental unit of society and that happy families are the foundation of a happy life. We recognize that every family looks different, and we passionately believe in helping all families find greater joy. To that end, we publish books for children and adults that invite families to live the Familius Ten Habits of Happy Family Life: love together, play together, learn together, work together, talk together, heal together, read together, eat together, laugh together, and give together.

Founded in 2012, Familius is located in Sanger, California.

Connect

Facebook: www.facebook.com/familiustalk

Twitter: @familiustalk, @paterfamilius1

Pinterest: www.pinterest.com/familius

Instagram: @familiustalk

FAMILIUS

"The most important work you ever do will be within the walls of your own home."